I've Got Issues!

Touching More Than The Hem

By Angela Lee-Easter

© 2018 by Angela Lee-Easter
Published by Your Destiny Productions Roanoke Rapids, NC 27870
Your Destiny Productions

Printed in the United States of America

All rights reserved. No part of this publication may be reproduced, stored in a retrieval system, or transmitted in any form or by any means- for example, electronic, photocopy, recording—without the prior written permission of the publisher. The only exception is brief quotations in printed reviews.

Lee-Easter. I've Got Issues! Touching More Than The Hem
https://www.facebook.com/identifyingthebrokenpieces/
angela.lee.easter@gmail.com
yourdestinyproductions2017@gmail.com
http://angelaleemoody.wixsite.com/destinyproductions
amazon.com/author/bylee_easter

Available at
amazon

Acknowledgments

*I acknowledge my husband, Rodney Darrell Easter,
Thanks for embracing my issues.*

Prologue

We are in a constant fight trying to find solutions to our problems. Unfortunately, as usual, we have put the cart before the horse. We cannot address our problems until we identify our issues. Our issues are the very things that motivate us to pursue the solution concerning what we are facing. If we could only develop a sense of urgency, about defining the issues that have captured us, then and only then will we as the people of God see clearly enough to solve our true problem. The true problem is that we are standing in the way of our destiny, as we unsuccessfully attempt to create paths to fulfilling God's plan for our lives.

Our paths are cloudy and cluttered with mistakes and blunders. We have become self-made problem solvers, who have no idea of our true purpose. God says come to me all of you who are heavy laden, and I will give you rest. He has given us a clear escape into his arms. Nevertheless, we have turned our heads seeking refuge elsewhere.

This book is designed to help the reader recognize the outstretched hand of God. He stands at the door waiting for us to realize he has designed our issues. We all have them, and the only way to solve the problems that are attached is to acknowledge and define their purpose. Each issue is designed for your success. We must embrace our purpose and move towards God's will. This elaborate dance is another way he has deliberately prepared us to win.

Table of Contents

You Are Smarter Than You Think How Smart Are You?

You Are a Genius

I've Got Issues

Big Issues Little Issues

Ostracized by My Issues

Embracing Your Issues Is the Only Way to Release Them

What is Your Problem?

Identify the Problem

Daddy Issues

The Problem is yours to Solve

It Just Does Not Add Up

Adding the Blessing; Taking away the Problem, Produces the Solution

Stop Blaming Everybody

It is Nothing Personal

Stop Hiding

Who Touched Me

What Kind of Touch Do You Have

The Helm is in Your Hand

Him and the Hem

My Issues are My Way Out

You Are Smarter Than You Think

For the wisdom of this world is foolishness with God. For it is written, He taketh the wise in their own craftiness" (I Corinthians 3:19, KJV).

Well, let me start by clarifying my position. I do not claim to be an expert in mathematics nor scientific calculations. I can barely understand the complexities involved in formulating and solving simplistic equations. Hence, I will leave such matters to the experts. However, it does not take a mathematician to identify issues and find justifiable solutions.

What defines a genius anyway? Well as Merriam Webster puts it, "a genius is extraordinary intellectual power especially as manifested in creative ability." If I were to put it in simple terms, it would describe a person that is very smart or gifted.

As related to this definition, one must ask the question; in what area must I demonstrate such actions? Often time people assume that knowing a little about a lot is considered a genius' characteristic. However, contrary to popular belief, that is just a know it all. A genius is categorized by his or her expertise in a particular area of study. This position may indicate an ability to identify solutions to simplify diverse problems.

To uncover your intellectual connection as a problem solver or an individual that simplifies the complexities of the impenetrable equation, you must prepare for struggle. There will be trial an error involved in your investigation. Therefore, persistence is an important component of the outcome. Of course, there will be times that you will want to throw in the towel, but you must resist. Your identification depends on staying your course.

So many people in the world are undiscovered geniuses. They are not aware of their intellect, nor, their creative ability. Often it takes a tragedy or a very difficult situation to occur in life before they are awakened to their strengths. We encounter geniuses every day. We may not classify them as such, but they are indeed highly intellectual and unique individuals.

Geniuses in their own right

Oprah Winfrey became a genius as a result of her life experiences. As a result of her issues, she was motivated to develop an industry that offered healing to broken and rejected people. Identifying her issues and solving her problems reached the masses and many were able to reach a resolution.

Tyler Perry also experienced tragedies in his life, that birth the genius in him. His struggles motivated him, and he created a way to connect to people as a storyteller, helping them in identifying with their life struggles. Joyce Meyers was raped, abused, and rejected, but as a result became a genius with love for all people. She has an overreaching capacity to touch wounded hearts through inspirational and testimonial messages.

Maya Angelo was raped, abused, and rejected as well; she became a genius, a world-renowned poet and author that learned to help other caged birds sing. Martin Luther King Jr. suffered at the hands of racism and social injustices but became a civil rights genius who changed the world and promoted equality. Tragedy and hard times, (issues) motivated each one of these heroes to become geniuses. They identified the very thing that aroused their intellect, and it inspired them to create solutions to their problems.

There is another woman that I believe to be an undiscovered genius. This woman inspired the writing of this book. A woman from the Bible who had undeniable issues; nevertheless, she was both smart and innovative. She understood all too well the complexities of multiplication, addition, division, and subtraction. She subtracted every penny from her account to pay her medical bills. She was left lacking, and her problem remained. *"And a woman having an issue of blood twelve years, which had spent all her living upon physicians, neither could be healed of any, came behind him, and touched the border of his garment: and immediately her issue of blood stanched"* (Luke 8:43-8, KJV).

However, when desperation and shame was an ever-occurring visitor, she decided to discontinue their relationship and leave them behind. She heard the excitement in the streets and soon discovered Jesus was passing by. She multiplied the thickness of her rags and ventured out with one thing on her mind. She went into public against the Laws' guidelines, but she realized this was an opportunity when she could finally confront her issues. As she, crawled on her knees, dividing the crowd, at last, she reached her destination. Her issues would motivate healing and virtue on this day. She stretched her body, reaching through the crowd of clutter dusty feet. She grabbed the hem of Jesus's garment; it was all that she could touch through the crowd. Her issue was the very thing that opened the door to her freedom. When this woman laid aside her embarrassment, shame, and fear, she was able to walk in her true identity; her issues no longer identified her. She made a difficult decision as she cleared her schedule that day and pressed toward the mark.

She positioned herself, on her knees crawling through the crowd, possibly stepped on, kicked, and pushed aside, but she refused to quit. She had a plan, and that was to get to Him, no, not his hem, but to Him. She realized the press of the people was too much for her weakened body. She got a glimpse and realized she was close enough to touch him. She stretched and strained, trying to work up the strength to keep on pressing, but the only thing she could touch was his hem. On this day she discovered that her issues were her motivation to find a solution, they were not her problem.

She was a genius crawling through the dusty streets of Galilee as she endured the growing urgency of the mob. Never minding the mob her focus was on Jesus. Only the power of the great physician could heal her condition. Her encounter with the Savior not only stopped the progression of her issue, but faith in him made her whole. This woman demonstrated the characteristics of a genius. Issues can produce your potential to become a genius.

Unless otherwise noted, all biblical passages referenced are from The Holy Bible, Authorized King James Version

How Smart Are You

To identify your intellectual capacity, you must first understand your issues. Identifying your issues and how they touch your life and others, is a start. Can you evaluate your issues, give the correct diagnosis and prescribe an accurate remedy? A highly intellectual individual spends a lot of time seeking to discover suitable solutions. What complexities are you facing? How can you solve or alleviate the problems that are attached to your issues?

Your ability to develop a strategy that will escort you into the presence of God is the measurement of your intelligence. You will no longer have the luxury of relying on others to provide you with the answer. God is expecting you to seek his face for the solution to the problems you are encountering. The lady with the issue of blood relied on the doctors to help her solve her issues. She realized after exhausting her finances, her natural dependencies were to no avail. At this point, she needed a doctor that would not charge her. I cannot tell you whether she believed in Jesus, before their encounter, but on this day, she believed and was healed. How smart you are, depends on what you do when Jesus is passing by.

You are a Genius

What classifies a person as a genius? In our natural mind, we have concluded that a genius refers to people such as Isaac Newton, Albert Einstein, and even Beethoven. Why have they been considered geniuses? These men dealt with some of the same issues we all face. They had problems that needed solutions. They would not allow their circumstances to defeat them. The thing that made them different was they designed a plan and was persistent.

The question that we must ask ourselves about an effective solution is; what is the first step? When considering the scientific method, the first step in finding a solution would be to make an observation. Well, the lady with the issue of blood, observed that her condition was not going to solve itself. She knew that she would probably have to live with it for the rest of her life. Therefore, she decided to search for a solution. Her first guess (hypothesis) was the doctors and the cost, which left her in the same condition and financial ruin. Her second-guess (hypothesis) was Jesus. Once she had a sensible hypothesis concerning her next step, she tested it, by touching Jesus. The data from this experiment was recorded in the Book of Luke, which is also an important step. The conclusion was obvious; she was healed immediately. The last step to the scientific method is replication. This step was replicated many times over throughout the Bible, and it is still proven true today.

I've Got Issues

Every day it seems as if we are faced with something new. Often, the new things are very familiar, a visitation from the past, that tends to present themselves in new ways. New ways to hurt and bruise us all over again. If we attempt to deny their existence, it will not rid us of their ability to scar. These are the issues that cling to us like an old worn out overcoat with the smells of long ago. It has become an addition to our everyday wardrobe. You may say, I have issues that are with me day after day, and they push and pull me in every direction. If I give in, I will be tossed with the waves of my circumstances. You must resist throwing in the towel. These issues will ruin your marriage, your friendships, and will eat away at your resolve. These issues seem to have ruined your life. You ask the question; how can they be beneficial? They are beneficial because they are the very thing that causes you to seek the help you need. Every overcomer has had issues.

There are people in this world today that are renowned. They would never have gotten to that status if it had not been for issues. Mahatma Gandhi was a man that faced major issues. Gandhi was India's Martin Luther King Jr. He fought for many freedoms for his people, resulting in his own taken away. In his early years, he was very shy and withdrawn, but he overcame those issues as he identified issues of greater concern. Issues are seasonal; they will linger until their purpose is manifested and their solution is proven successful. Gandhi was put in jail because of political issues, which demonstrated inequality and social injustices. He fought to put an end to unfair treatment of his people. Issues may not always motivate a solution for you but may end the suffering of others.

    Harriet Tubman also had issues. Her issues were directly connected to freedom. Her issues insisted that all men should be free. As a result, she put her life in harm's way seeking to gain those freedoms for men, women, and children that were enslaved. You may soon realize that issues come in various forms, which are connected directly to you but may involve the outcome of others. If you are smart enough, you will seek methods that will break the chains of captivity and provide a way of escape. What issues bound you and what methods will you use to gain your freedom?

Big Issues Little Issues

Issues come in all sizes, but the size often differs depending on the perception of who is involved. As individuals, we view our situations and determine the size based on our personal experiences. We never consider others' issues in the evaluation of our situation. Our issue may initially be a molehill, but our emotional attachments magnify it, and it may become a mountain of your own making. Our connections make the urgency of the solution paramount.

Your issue may be small, but because you are having a personal meltdown, it has become your giant. It is not to say that you have exaggerated or blown things out of proportion. It is just your interpretation or perception of what you are facing. The size of your issue is not a measurement used by God to decide whether to come to your aid. The awesome thing about the God we serve is there is no issue too big or too small.

God sees the need of his child. As natural parents it does not matter whether our child has a scrape, cut, or a break, we are equally concerned with their well-being. We must never underestimate the love of God; we could never compete with that. *"Or what man is there of you, whom if his son asks bread, will he give him a stone. If ye then, being evil, know how to give good gifts unto your children, how much more shall your Father which is in heaven give good things to them that ask him"* (Matt. 7:9, 11, KJV)?

Take note, the greater the issue, the greater the anointing to follow. Remember with God things are not as they are with a natural man. You could be facing a small issue with a big attachment; likewise, there could be a big issue with a small attachment. This may be very confusing, but consider for a moment, a car accident that results in the car being totaled but the passenger only suffering a scratch. On the other hand, a bike accident that scrapes the paint off the handle, but the rider hits his head and dies. Big issues can have small outcomes, and small issues can have big outcomes. The outcome of an issue can be miniscule or catastrophic. The issue is not your major concern, but the outcome is. Do not be trapped in the issue; it is not the problem; it is a means to a solution.

Big or small, your issue is your motivation to pursue a positive outcome. Never become overwhelmed with an issue, making it a permanent fixture, rather keep it a fleeting circumstance, which promotes a greater level. I want to encourage you to focus more on God's intentions and less on your temporary position. *"While we look not at the things which are seen, but at the things which are not seen: for the things which are seen are temporal; but the things which are not seen are eternal" (2 Corn. 4:18, KJV).* God has an eternal goal for you and your issues are of no matter. No matter the size you are being led in the direction of eternity.

Ostracized by Issues

Nobody wants to be friends with people who have issues. That is why people are quick to hide them. They rather crawl through the crowd avoiding nasty looks and the wagging fingers. They know the results of exposing their issues. Issues have caused many people to be addicted to prescription medications. Medications help to dull out the realization of what they are facing. Just like the woman with the issue of blood, she used all her money looking for medicines to rid her of her issue, but the money did her no good nor the remedy. There's only one way to stop the issues, you must become a problem solver, a true genius: be smart, be creative, and be diligent.

One true characteristic of a genius is persistence. You must press through, no matter who or what stands in your way. The Creator of heaven and earth has empowered you, and he is all wise and all knowing. His intellectual capacity is beyond man's comprehension. You can do all things through Christ who has strengthened you. It may be a lonely road for a while, but you will have the opportunity to work without distractions during your time of resolution. It is only a season. It is true you may be pushed away, counted out, and discarded, but you must press your way until you have reached Him.

Jesus is waiting for you to make a move. Just know it is (Him) who wears the hem that heals your issues. Those you lost during the difficulties of your problems may never return. Those you gained will always remain.

God will appoint the right people to accompany you through this journey. Their appointments and assignments are designed with purpose. However, the unnecessary weight of people without purpose in your life will hold you back. But when you connect with Him, nothing can prevent your destiny. Never be ashamed of your issues they are what got you here.

Embracing Your Issues is the Only Way to Release Them

Now that you see your issues as a necessary part of your deliverance, you can move forward knowing that all things are working for your good. God has your outcome in his hands, and as long as you depend on and trust him, you will be in his favor. When you acknowledge your issues and identify them as the solution to finding your truth, your call, and your destiny, you will be free to move to the next level. Embrace your struggles, embrace your hurts, and embrace each pain you have encountered.

Your issues are only a temporary embrace that prepares you for release. Each encounter equips you with the tools you will need as you develop your spiritual muscles. You are no longer in captivity as a result of what you have experienced. You are now in a position to embrace the next level as you walk with God. Each time you release you will find yourself facing a new challenge. You are stronger now that you have realized the process of your spiritual maturation. You are a spiritual intellectual; you can no longer rely on natural understanding. Now that you have a spiritual understanding of what is required, you will have to comply with that knowledge. Your compliance will require complete obedience.

    If you are to continue to experience the freedoms attached to your spiritual intellect, you will have to embrace the only thing that can promote the release, which is your issues.

What is your Problem?

We all have issues; there are individual solutions to them all. However, if we are walking in denial, we will never experience the indicator of deliverance. What is an issue, and what is the true representation of an issue? Well, an issue is a situation that requires a constructive solution to eliminate its ability to prevent, to hold back development, and isolate. Simply put, an issue is not a problem.

Now, the problem can come in many forms. It could be in the form of doubt. Maybe you doubt what you have been called to do. You find it hard to believe that God could use someone like you. You view yourself as someone that has a history, which is stained with sin and shame. You are aware of the call on your life, but you are too ashamed to walk in it. You feel that people will point their fingers in disapproval.

What is your problem? Your problem is you have not forgiven yourself. If God said it and ordained it, your past should not be a factor. In God's eyes, you are clean, and the Blood of Jesus is responsible for your justification. Issues will always be a part of our lives as born-again believers, and they will occur before and after Christ. We will continue to encounter issues, which will provide the training needed to step out of our unworthiness into the worth of Christ. There is a solution to the problem of unforgiveness, and that solution is in the faith to believe God for validation. Validation is not in the hands of man but the heart of God.

He cleansed you from all unrighteousness and made you an heir to the kingdom. God has endorsed your call. He has put you in a position that cannot be questioned by a man. Therefore, do not doubt your call or your position for it was given and ordained by Him. He chose you for such a time as this. You are the one that will set the scene for souls to come into the Kingdom, not subject to condemnation, but accepted in love. You are asking why me? Your testimony is a personal reference verifying that you are capable of fulfilling the job's requirements. You are the candidate with the job experience to do what is necessary to win the lost. You can identify with their struggle. You can sympathize with their hurts, and you are passionate about their souls. Your problem and your issue have made you the perfect vessel to be filled with

God's love, to share with the lost. You are Qualified.

Identify the Problem

How do you identify the problem? The first thing you must understand is the issue is not the problem. The thing that you are confronted with is the problem. The issue is the motivation to find a solution. The issue may be your husband the problem may be alcoholism, or your issue may be your child, but the problem may be disobedience. What is its impact on your current position? You must find a way to address its effects, which requires identification.

Now that you understand how to define an issue and identify a problem, you can take the necessary steps, which will direct you towards your destiny. Identifying the problem is also an important step in developing your effectiveness. Your ministry depends on this identification. The success of your marriage depends on the definition of your issues. Without this process, you will be trapped in a stagnated place. You will have a difficult time trying to operate in ministry with unresolved problems and unidentified issues.

Your levels of development depend on the success in the process. God has provided you with what is needed to reach your goals. However, you must be cognizant of what is in plain sight. The Lord has ordered your steps and illuminated your pathway. You cannot afford to miss the signs he is sending, if so you will delay the process. The problem is a necessary component; it is a building block in the completion of your temple. "Know ye not that ye are the temple of God, and *that* the

Spirit of God dwelleth in you" *(1 Corinthians 3:16, KJV)?*

Daddy Issues

Let's get real. Many of our issues did not appear overnight. They were a process that dragged on for years. Therefore, we will not find an over-night solution. The best way to find a resolution is the process of backward reasoning. You must see the end and work your way back to the beginning. In doing so, you will identify every step in the process, never to repeat it.

My Issues originated from many encounters I experienced through life. However, one issue I can identify was my daddy issues. As a result, of daddy issues, I became a hard woman. I did not like men telling me what to do even if it was asked nicely. I never wanted another man to dominate me, control, or abuse me again. I recognized this at a very young age.

My father left us and returned several times until my mom had, had enough. When he was there, he beat us, cursed us, and neglected us. I remember when he learned about homemade tattooing, he practiced on us all, except for the ones who were afraid of the needle. Their resistance got them a good tongue lashing though. Nevertheless, out of six children about three of us were branded, I was only in third grade during the process.

As a teenager, he was long gone, but his mark remained. I wore it through high school, the prom, and graduation. It was there in my first and second marriage and both divorces. Was I a marked woman, with the instructions for other men to repeat the action of my father?

Was it a symbol that the women in my life could not have a good marriage? Although it seems true, I knew better.

My daddy issues resulted in my motivation. That motivation directed me into the arms of a loving, forgiving, and eternal daddy that would erase the brand my natural father gave and replace it with his love. Today the tattoo is still there but forever covered with the words BLESSED. Because of my daddy issues, I am blessed. My daddy is old now and can hardly remember what I will never forget, but because of his actions, I became a strong, powerful, but submissive woman of God. I love my daddy; he bears the burdens, the pains, and the guilt of the past, I would never increase his suffering by pushing him away. My heavenly father has shown me, love, I have never known. His love has shown me how to be a wife, a mother, and a child. Yes, a child, that is loved and allowed to play in the safety of his eternal glory. The brand on my skin does not matter, whether the marks are of tattoo ink, belts, or switches, my soul is spotless, for His blood has cleansed me.

The Problem is yours to Solve.

One thing that most people do not want to admit is that they have a problem. Having a problem is not a bad thing. The bad thing is when the problem has you. Learning how to label or identify a problem properly is key to elevating your position. This is the intended result. Often Christians, hold on to problems as if they are biologically connected to it. Problems are not intended to reside indefinitely with you. They are temporary fires to jolt you into your birthrights.

It is true your problem is yours and design to suit you to a tee. The intended outcome is for you alone. You see, although your problems may be identical to others, it will not have the same outcome. Not many will have the mental capacity to understand the dynamics of this process. Nonetheless, the lack of understanding does not outweigh the command of obedience. Obey God's instructions concerning this process, and the outcome will be in your favor.

This problem is yours, and you are required to seek out a solution. Once you realize that the problem is working for your good, the solution will come rather easily. The problem most people have in this instance is they look beyond the situation and create a scenario that develops into a mountain instead of the existing molehill.

You have to see the problem for what it is and not what it can be. You can solve a problem once you add up its true purpose. Think about Balaam and his donkey; he had a problem. *"And the ass saw the angel of the LORD standing in the way, and his sword drawn in his hand: and the ass turned aside out of the way and went into the field: and Balaam smote the ass, to turn her into the way" (Numbers 22:23, KJV).* Balaam was angry and frustrated, but when he realized why the problem existed, out of fear he became the solution. His heart was not right, and his plans was contrary. But when he heard the voice of God, he followed his instruction.

It Just Does Not Add Up

You have evaluated your situation. You have identified the problem. You have even embraced the issue, but it just does not add up. The issue, the problem, and the solution have you in a whirlwind. The manifestation of your resolve has been delayed. Standing still and allowing the process will be the only way to reach your expected end. You will have to exhibit some patience during this ordeal. If you are seeking a specific result, you will have to have a perfect mixture of patience and persistence.

This situation is not adding up because you are not implementing a supernatural mathematical formula. You are using a natural resolution expecting a spiritual outcome. The natural man subtraction leaves one lacking, however with God's methods of subtraction the results are always multiplied. If you subtract sin from your life, God promises to give you an abundant life. He will multiply your blessings if you follow his plan. It will add up if you use God's tools of calculation. As the people of God, we often have relied on our abilities to rationalize and examine our issues under a microscope of our design. It is impossible to examine what is of God with what man has designed. The mind must be transformed; the thought process must be adjusted. God thoughts and ways are very different from that of man. Therefore, we must acknowledge that God has specific steps that must be taken to understand the path he has for us.

When you look at his plan, you will observe that God had everything in place before you ever showed up. All things make sense when seen through the eyes of God. If you would take the time to add up his promises, his love, and his forgiveness, there will be no doubts concerning his plan. The plan was predestined with you in mind. Everything is in place so that you will experience his favor. You must stop trying to figure it out on your own. God has an appointed time when he will reveal it to you. Your lack of understanding as it relates to how things add up, will not prevent what God has prepared for you. If you obey him, prepare to receive what he has promised in your season he will provide a clear path for you to follow. Many things that you have encountered have appeared to be far from that path, but trust and believe God was working it out for your good. Everything is adding up, now prepare for the overflow.

Adding the Blessing, Taking away the Problem, Produces the Solution

Adding up the blessings is the first step to breaking free from the curse of lies. Yes, lies. Who is lying? Well, I want you to know Satan hates to see you blessed. He lost ground when you start confessing what the Lord was doing in your life. His goal was to keep you complaining and doubting. He has to put an end to your joy, your peace, and your prosperity. If you notice I said, your joy, your peace, and your prosperity. It belongs to you. God has destined you to walk in his promises.

However, the accuser, the false witness, and the murderer have planned defeat for you.

You cannot allow him space. You must recognize what God has done and what he is continuing to do. Your job is to make your declaration daily that God will be exalted, and your enemies will be scattered. My dear Christian fellow, it is up to you to win the fight. God has given you every defensive weapon needed to come out with the victory. The greatest weapon you have is PRAISE! Now, let us add up the blessings. Look at your life; I am sure you can find countless reasons to complain.

    Nevertheless, I can guarantee that your blessing outweighs every complaint. Every morning God gives us a wrapped gift. We have no idea what is in this beautiful presentation of love. However, when we open it, there is no rush, but we must savor every moment of its glory, as we experience a new day. What an awesome blessing. It is a moment in time we have never experienced. The smells, tastes, feelings, observations, and sounds are all new.

    It is an opportunity to do better than the day before. It is a day to love and to forgive. It is a day to seek out the beauty and share it with others. Just for a moment, stand in the sun with your eyes closed, clearing the mind, and breathe deeply. Taking the time to appreciate the blessings will develop a spirit of gratefulness. This mental exercise will subtract the problem and multiply the blessings. Often, we miss what is right in front of us because of our failure to appreciate life. What is the problem? Distractions produce deafness and blindness. Satan has designed a wall of deception that blocks what is right in front of you. How can you remove what you do not acknowledge? The solution is found in awareness. You cannot expect to win a race if you are not aware of your position. The finish line is closer than you think. None of your runnings has been in vain. Your participation in this race has a divine purpose. Your reward will be worth it all, in this life, and in the one to come. Remember if you keep your eyes on the Lord, he will lead you on the right path and that path is where you will discover the solution.

Stop Blaming Everybody

Okay, I get it. Your mom was not there. Your father walked out when you were very young. No one understands you. Life has been hard. You had to fend for yourself. Nobody was ever there for you. I get it, trust me, you were abused, rejected, denied, and even abandoned.

But, now it is time to put those things behind you and trust God for the rest of the way. If you continue to focus on the pain and hurt of your past, you will never be able to move forward. All the promises of God are forward. He has left nothing in your past that you need to go back and retrieve. Your blessings and prosperity are in your future.

I know it is hard because it was hard for me. Everything that I had faced, I would talk about, I used it as a crutch which prevented forward motion. When I realize what I was missing and what God had in store for me, I let go, I had to let it all go. It did not happen overnight, but gradually I released. I could no longer blame people for where I was or where I had not gone. They were not holding me back; it was me. I agreed that they did some hurtful and hateful things in my past. However, the hate and hurt have been left where it happened, in my past.

It is my job to help heal and not worsen the pains of the past. The past created issues, but those same issues have created paths fulfilling my purpose. Issues should push you forward not hold you back. The lady with the issue of blood pushed through the crowd until she found her deliverance. Push Pass the Pain and embrace your future.

It Is Nothing Personal

Having issues can be misconstrued at times as personal. People may accuse you of having problems with them. As a result, you may suffer unsolicited attacks. Leaving you to bandage scars that were inflicted due to misinterpretation. During this time of conflict, you will notice a shift in companions and associates. This season has run its course and now requires dismissal. The dismissal of old relationships and the acceptance of new ones will position you in the perfect Will of God. I know you are wondering why is this necessary. Your old companions have gone as far as they can go. The design of this new relationship is, to accompany you through the next stage of the journey.

There may be a period of this transition when you will experience loneliness. Nevertheless, this is to be expected. You must rely on God. It does not matter how people feel or how they react to your issues, remember God will allow issues to produce the healing you need. The healing, as with the lady with the issue of blood will position you in right standing with God.

You will have the favor of God to go places you were denied. The devourer will no longer have access to your resources. You will plant, produce, and deliver. Your issue had left you barren, but in this season, you will be fruitful, and you will multiply. It is because you no longer see issues as a punishment for failures. You are in a spiritual place where you understand it is nothing personal, whether it's you or others' thoughts concerning you; it is your opportunity to grow.

Stop Hiding

One, Two, Three, ready or not here I come. I remember playing hiding-go-seek when I was a child. It was a fitting game for my age. If hiding is, still a game that is played, it is a sign of immaturity. It also signifies a fear of exposure. Running from the past will not rid you of its stains nor its stench. The only way to win is to stop running and face the thing that haunts you.

When you face the past and its fading ability to hold you, hostage, you will no longer have to run. Your face-to-face encounter will substantiate your power over past activities. Your mistakes, shortcomings, and failures will be powerless against your new position. Your new position has cleared the path; now you can run. Your running is no longer in vain. The only hiding place that exists is under the wings of the all mighty. *"Thou art my hiding place; thou shalt preserve me from trouble; thou shalt compass me about with songs of deliverance. Selah." (Psalms 32:7, KJV).*

In God, you are free to live the life he intended without interruptions. Your exposure is a testimony that God will deliver those who surrender to his love. You are hidden but not afraid you are under God's protection.

Psalms 91

He that dwelleth in the secret place of the highest shall abide under the shadow of the Almighty.

I will say of the LORD; He is my refuge and my fortress: my God; in him will I trust.

Surely, he shall deliver thee from the snare of the fowler, and from the noisome pestilence.

He shall cover thee with his feathers, and under his wings shalt thou trust: his truth shall be thy shield and buckler (Psalms 91, KJV).

God has predestined your safety. The person whom you have become is no mystery to him. You are exactly where you should be, and that position is vital to Kingdom Building. Your obedience and willingness are important to the move of God. You were birth into this world equipped by God to do the work. Everything that you have been through has prepared you for this task. It may look hard in the beginning, but when you step out and start the work, you will realize it wears as a tailored suit, designed just for you. Yes, indeed this is your destiny. What would have taken months or even years of training to accomplish, you have grasped immediately. This is because you were designed to do it. You must not allow fear to overshadow your God-given gifts and talents. You must not stand in the way of your destiny. Now get busy doing what you were created to do. No one can stop you, God ordained it.

Who Touched Me

Throughout the New Testament, we read and study how Jesus touched people lives in so many ways. He touched their brokenness. He touched their loneliness. He touched the hunger and thirsts. Jesus even touched them in death, such as Lazarus and Jairus daughter. His touch has the power to transform lives and give them a clearer perspective. The lady caught in adultery; life was changed in such a way that what she valued before meeting Jesus, no longer held the same value. Legion would never forget the man that cast out the demons and freed him from his bondage. And could we ever forget the disciples, they all laid down their former lives to follow Jesus? His touch is beyond physical human contact.

Jesus healing was in his hands, as well as in his loving Words. "And they bring unto him one that was deaf and had an impediment in his speech, and they beseech him to put his hand upon him." *(Mark 7:32, KJV)*. Jesus said to him, "Shall I come and heal him?" The centurion replied, "Lord, I do not deserve to have you come under my roof. But just say the word, and my servant will be healed." *(Matthew 8:7-8, KJV)*. His love was able to reach the deep places. He knew healing was not enough. He knew that one must be made whole to experience true freedom from captivity.

Jesus was doing the work of him who sent him. It was his job to serve the people. He did not mind the issues nor the problems.

The issues were motivation for the people to seek a solution, and he was the answer to their problem.

One day as Jesus was walking the streets of Galilee, crowded with people pushing and pressing to reach him, felt something strange but familiar. The very actions would take place when he would touch the sick, the leopard, the dying. However, he was not touching anyone, and powerful healing was activated and flowing out from him. He knew then it had to be a touch. He asked who touched me. It was the lady with the issue. Your issue provides access to Jesus.
He wants to heal you. He came to heal you. Who can touch Jesus? Desperation, loneliness, cancer, and death touches Jesus. The touch will remove the pain, the hurt, and the sting.

The beautiful thing about Jesus is he does not mind you touching him.

"And she stood at his feet behind *him* weeping, and began to wash his feet with tears, and did wipe *them* with the hairs of her head, and kissed his feet, and anointed *them* with the ointment" *(Luke 7:38, KJV)*. No matter how you touch him, it will be life-changing. The thief on the cross-touched him with his faith, and that day he went to paradise. Touch him, and you will experience the fullness of his power.

What Kind of Touch Do You Have?

Many people in the church are looking for a touch. They will even sing songs describing their desire to experience his touch within the congregation. *"He Touched Me."* What would I like to know is what kind of touch do you have? As people of God, we must stop this desperate search for a touch and be prepared to give one.

The lady with the issue of blood was a perfect example that we can touch as well. If our touch of faith can make a difference to Jesus, it can also make a difference to his people. Let our lives reach out and touch those with issues. Let us be the givers this time.

We must stop looking for a handout and start giving a hand. Let us look for opportunities to be a blessing. We are to be the doctors and nurses that God uses to administer the necessary healing to the hurting. Those that are sick need the faith and the healing hands of the believers. It stands true that it is more blessed to give than to receive.

For some reason, many have forgotten the importance of helping others. Many of the so-called men and women of God are calling meetings where they can raise a collection. Why are there no meetings called to just blessed the people and not ask for anything?

The Hem is in Your Hand

Your healing is in your hands. Everything we need to be made whole is right in front of us, but because it did not come the way we expected it we reject it. Unfortunately, this rejection has kept you at the Pool of Bethesda. You are waiting for the waters to be trouble and the Living Water is standing before you. You are so adamant about the waters of Bethesda you have asked the Living waters to move aside; because he is blocking your access.

Unfortunately there is a sad truth. You are so blind believing your way is the right way you will die waiting for something that will never happen. Until you realize he is the way, the truth, and the life, your waiting will always be in vain. The hem is in your hand, but Christ should be in your heart. We must not worship the creation we must worship the Creator. *"They traded the truth about God for a lie. So, they worshiped and served the things God created instead of the Creator himself, who is worthy of eternal praise! Amen"* *(Roman 1:25, NIV).*

Your path is set, and your destiny is sure. However, you cannot lose focus. You must keep your eyes on Jesus and not the things surrounding you. Everyone has their part to play, and their parts only represent a small portion of assisting you in the direction God is leading. If you are too attached to the hem, you will become a part of the fabric. If this is the case, you will never become the wearer only the toucher. He wants you to wear

the robe. "I counsel thee to buy of me gold tried in the fire, that thou mayest be rich; and white raiment, that thou mayest be clothed, and *that* the shame of thy nakedness do not appear; and anoint thine eyes with eyesalve, that thou mayest see" (*Revelation 3:18, KJV*).   Release the hem and put on a God-designed robe;
it will cover your sickness, your hurt, and your sin. Your sickness and hurt have been a result of your doubt and unbelief. Everything you need to be made whole has been designed and made ready by God the Father. He desires that you reach your predestined position, and it is going to take your trusting in him.

Him and the Hem

Often because of tradition, people fail to realize that there are easier ways to reach a solution. Unfortunately, because of familiarity and comfort, they continue to walk in the same direction, which delays their destiny. We live in a day and time that the world is constantly changing. We cannot continue to rely on the ways of yesteryears. Don't get me wrong, God's Word will never change, however; the presentation may come in different forms.

Will you reject the Word because the presenter is of a different race, gender, religion, or age? We must remove ourselves from the mold of tradition. The scriptures say to us let this mind be in you that was also in

Christ Jesus. God wants us to have a new mind.

Mistaken Identity

My name is more than what you call me. My name is more than identification. I am much more than what your eyes observe. You may look at me and develop a mental profile to try to satisfy your curiosity. Unfortunately, an in-depth investigation will only come up short. I am more than what you can ever imagine. No amount of research will reveal the complexity of who God has ordained me to be. There's purpose in the hidden. God always waits until the fullness of time has come before he reveals his plan.

To be perfectly honest I cannot begin to explain this hidden mystery. If I could, it would be solving secrets of old. My existence and purpose have been hidden in God from the beginning. If I could solve this mystery, I would be seeing into the mind of God. You see he is not finished with me yet. Therefore, my explanation would be a whimsical attempt to know his plans.

Patience is the key to this mystery. Waiting for his perfect timing without interrupting the process will guarantee the plan's success. To know who I am and who God has to purpose me to be, I must be still and allow him to put all things in its proper place. All I can say with surety is that I am so much more and so are you.

My Issues, My Way Out

My issues have been my motivation. They have pushed me to press toward the mark for the prize of the high calling of God in Christ Jesus. If it had not been for my issues, I would have never become a writer, teacher, or a businessperson. Issues are not the problem, but the motivation is leading to the solution. My marriage was the issue, and the problem was unfaithfulness.

The marriage was not the problem, his unfaithfulness was, which in turn destroyed the marriage. The solution must be the desire of both parties. Otherwise, the results will be unfruitful. Healing can only come when the underlined truth is revealed. The open door that leads to the solution is always available. However, many pretend not to see the answer because they will have given up the very thing that is causing the problem. The only way out is to let go. Familiarity and comfort can sometimes prolong the pain. The issue will always exist as long as the problem persists. As the people of God, we are responsible for representing Jesus and what he would do. The issues he faced when on earth he did not allow to sway him from doing the will of God. This is our resolve as well; we cannot allow our situation to put the work of the Kingdom on hold. If we truly want to experience the freedoms of God, walking in his liberty, we must identify the issue and use it to guide us to our deliverance.

It Is Time to Go Up

Once you have identified the issue and used it to solve the problem, you can rise. There are higher heights and deeper depths in understanding the will of God for your life. Unfortunately, when your mind is cluttered with the world around you, there is no room to move. The movement after freedom is only in one direction, and the direction will result in elevation. The question that always remains is, are you ready to take a leap of faith towards your destiny? Your issues have brought you to the valley of decision. Will you mope around undecisive or will you go higher?

Moses had issues with the Israelites complaining, accusing him of failing them and bringing them out of Egypt to die. God's solution to the problem of their rebellion was to meet him on the mountain. He had to go to a higher place to get an answer. God did not remove the issue but created a solution that could be applied, to build the people's faith. Although the people continued to return to their old ways, Moses trusted God and continued to commune with him in the mountain, where he grew stronger and found solutions.

Often time the solution is beyond your reach, that is if you remain in your present position. The answer to your problem will require you to seek higher ground. The lady with the issue of blood, healing was out of her reach as long as she depended on natural solutions. She had to go beyond her level of understanding and operate at a higher level of faith.

About the Author

Angela has dedicated her life to fulfilling Gods plans concerning winning the lost to Christ. Writing has been her passion for many years. She uses this tool to reach hearts and homes with her testimonies and purposeful experiences. Through her life, she has had to face tragedy, pains, and failures, but through it all, God has kept her. She writes this book in hopes that the readers will understand that the race is not given to the swift nor the strong, but to the one that endures to the end. Are you strong enough is not a question related to natural strength, it relates to one's spiritual ability.

She encourages others to never give up in this race. She believes it is our heavenly duty to stand at arms, as we defend the weak and shattered, remembering we were in their shoes not long ago. Angela writes her life and experiences uniquely and comprehensively. Her practical application to staying strong even when weaknesses are all around, derived from her biblical perspective. Which is to trust in God with all your heart and lean not to your own understanding. She is strong enough for the season in which she stands, prepared to fight the good fight of faith.

www.ingramcontent.com/pod-product-compliance
Lightning Source LLC
Chambersburg PA
CBHW071330040426
42444CB00009B/2125